Petalouda

Aspasia Fotakis

Presentation by *BookLeaf Publishing*

Web: www.bookleafpub.com

E-mail: info@bookleafpub.com

ISBN: 9789357441407

First edition 2023

Butterfly

Her wings no longer feel wet and heavy
The sun no longer hurts her skin
Her soul has slowed its search for the unknown
Her mind races to find peace.

Darlin'

You taught her that she did not lose,
because one only loses when something of worth
is lost.
And you my darlin', have shown the world that
your worth is nothing more than less.

Soul

And if he asked if she still loved him, she would
say yes.
And if he asked her why, she would say because
she believed in him and believed in them,
And if he asked her how, she would say,
Because when you have a soul like hers, no
matter how much you try to not believe, you just
can't stop.

Emerging

Her feet no longer felt like they were falling into
quick sand
Her legs no longer felt like they were noodles
attempting to hold up a six story building
Her heart no longer felt like it was scattered
across the city
She knew she was slowly emerging from the
world that had crumbled on top of her.

Parallel

I woke up in a parallel Universe
Seeing myself move through this familiar life
but being unfamiliar to it
Watching the characters around me wearing the
faces of friends and loved ones who were now
strangers to me
Sitting in my apartment unsure of where I am
Moving through each day on mute, noises and
voices all around me drowned out under water
Looking at my reflection wondering who the sad
woman looking back at me is
Sorting through the events like giant puzzle
pieces that just didn't fit
Wondering when I was taken out of my life and
placed into this parallel Universe with the same
people and surroundings which were now
unknown to me
I only knew one thing before I awoke in this
parallel Universe
You left and you never said goodbye.

Reflection

The pillow no longer showed the wet of her tears
Her reflection no longer showed her sadness
The silence no longer seemed so loud.

Beautifully Broken

And all her broken pieces put together, shined like those of a disco ball.

Universe

The Universe speaks to you, and when you
refuse to hear it,
The Universe will show you.
And when you refuse to see it, The Universe
will break you.
And when you want to give up, the Universe
will rebuild you.

Fairytale

When her Fairytale vanished,
She looked around at her reality
Lost without a map
Searching for the Prince that left her
Only to find she was the Queen.

Stand

Ever notice how heavy it feels to stand?
How heavy your body feels when you carry all
the weight?
How your legs feel like they are going to just
give out right where you are standing, because
you so desperately need to just lie down, curl up,
and drift off into a sleep so you can wake up and
sigh because it was all just a bad dream?

Paint

Paint the smile on your face,
Wipe the tear before it drips down your cheek
and reveals the screams hidden underneath that
smile.

Torn

Life is a series of events that tears you in two
leaving you walking on the border of your
reality and your nightmares.
Walking through your new reality after a
heartbreak, but stuck in the dense fog of why
and how.
Being present in a friendship, but torn with the
changes that have emerged like weeds that
refuse to leave.
Smiling through each day, but torn with the
anxiety, sadness, screams, and tears that teeter
on your lips every time you open your mouth.
Knowing you should be angry and filled with
disdain, but torn with sadness and yearning,
searching in the fog for the hand that left you
there.

One Country, Two Worlds

We exist in one country but we live in two
different worlds.
There's the world of rugs piled high with
everything that's been shoved under them,
And there's the world of rugs stained with blood
and tears for reasons mankind has no good
answer for.
There's the world where walking down the street
is as simple as that,
And there's the world where walking down the
street could be ones last walk, for a reason as
simple as the act of walking down the street.
There's the world where doors open effortlessly,
And there's the world where doors are bolted
shut for reasons that leave a bitter taste in one's
mouth.
There's the world where rules don't apply,
And there's the world where the smallest rule
broken leads to punishment of a thousand deaths
for reasons that sound like incomplete sentences.
There's the world where people see you, hear
you, speak to you, respect you,
And there's the world where people only see
color and labels.
There's the world that is blind,

And there's the world that hasn't stopped
marching.
Which world do you live in?

Say

My voice has been silenced and shushed
My voice has been ridiculed, criticized, and
laughed at
My voice has been ignored, tuned out, a mere
humming noise in the background
My voice has been pushed down, shut away, told
to go to sleep
My voice has been told it won't be heard
My voice has been told its important
My voice has been told why don't you ever
speak up
My voice has been told you don't know what
you're talking about
My voice has been told it holds weight
My voice has been told it needs to be heard
My voice only knows how to scream
My voice only knows to be heard when it's loud
My voice knows it only falls on deaf ears
My voice is tired
My voice is fighting
My voice is ready
My voice is coming
My voice will be heard

2 AM

It's 2 AM and I'm wide awake asleep,
Replaying the haunting memories as if on fast
forward 8x's speed.
Flashes of laughter, silliness, eyes rolling, loud
silence, cuddling, playing, screaming, begging,
bitterness, sweetness, emptiness, flooding my
memory bank.
Quick bursts of Flashes.
Wide awake asleep at 2 AM.

World

The world is burning,
Don't worry I captured the picture.
The hatred is spreading,
Don't worry I sent my thoughts and prayers.
The drugs are overpowering,
Don't worry we're working on a new one.
The guns are exploding,
Don't worry the children know the drill.
The people have given up,
Don't worry Uncle Sam is watching.
The war of color is flooding the streets with
rivers of red,
Don't worry the parade of blue will clean it up.
The humanity is lost,
Don't worry we never had it.

Unlovable Beauty

You're so beautiful
Thank you
You have such a great heart
Thank you
You're such a sweetheart
Thank you
You're so sexy
Thank you
You deserve the world
Thank you
The world was taken not given, her beauty
attracted temporary not forever, and her good
heart beaten.

Ex-Lover

Dear Ex-Lover,

Thank you for shattering me into a million pieces. Breaking my heart piece by piece like a crystal vase. Leaving me to search for and find the million little pieces, so I can put them back together with a beautiful gold outline.

Thank you for breaking me and allowing all the brokenness in me to make me that much more human, that much more delicate, that much more beautiful.

For the strength I have found within me that I never knew I had until you shattered every piece of me.
For awakening me to my power as a woman, and teaching me that it will never be taken from me again.
For bringing out the gold in me that will shine every beautiful flaw for the world to see.
For the warrior in me that will fight for myself because I have never loved myself as much as I do now.
For my voice that will resonate loud for all to hear.

For showing me that the only person I need to make happy is the warrior woman looking back at me in the mirror.

So thank you ex- lover for I would have never fallen in love with my crown if you didn't fall out of love with me.

Peace & Love,

Warrior Woman

Kima

She knew she survived the wave this time
She knew she was given the strength of her
ancestors
She understood her value and purpose
She knew she had an army of warriors walking
beside her
She knew this wouldn't be the last wave
She knew she could survive them now

Silence

Silence so loud she must stay busy to drown it
out
Silence so loud it keeps her awake at night
Silence so loud she watches the thoughts race
through her mind like she's in slow motion while
everything around her is speeding
Silence so loud she yearns for peace but only
finds chaos
Silence so loud she begs for it to be quiet so she
can forget
Silence so loud it consumes her until she is
falling down the rabbit hole like Alice only she
never reaches Wonderland.

Warrior Women

Warriors have the strength of armies
Warriors carry the weight of the world every
second of every day
They are put in the shadows of men for the
world is scared of the power they hold
They are silenced for the fear of their voices
resonating
They are told their bodies are never perfect and
never enough for the comfort of keeping them
apart because they are too powerful united
They are told they are too sexy for the protection
of weak men that can't control themselves
They are told to prove themselves for the sake of
the male ego
They are survivors, fighters, healers, protectors,
creators
They are warriors.
They are us.
They are women.

www.ingramcontent.com/pod-product-compliance
Lightning Source LLC
LaVergne TN
LVHW050307200726

843509LV00015B/3202